& North Wales

by Paul Shannon & John Hillmer

Past and
Present

Past & Present Publishing Ltd

ALTON TOWERS: On August 19 1961 (right), Fowler 2-6-4T No. 42323 calls at the very attractive station at Alton Towers with the 11.25am Leek-Uttoxeter local service. Located on the North Staffordshire Railway's erstwhile Churnet Valley line, the station has happily survived and is now one of the finest examples of restored railway architecture in the area under review. The station is pictured (below) in 1988. *Michael Mensing/PDS.*

CONTENTS

FRONT COVER:
BIRKENHEAD WOODSIDE: Birkenhead's possibilities for development were recognised early in the 19th century because of its proximity to Liverpool, albeit on the opposite bank of the River Mersey. A ferry crossing dates back to the Middle Ages, when Monks from Birkenhead Priory were granted the franchise. A steam-boat commenced operations from Woodside in 1822 and in 1840 the Chester & Birkenhead Railway opened. This company was taken over jointly in 1860 by the GWR and the LNWR, who realised that the original Monk's ferry terminus was inadequate, and in any case the Woodside Ferry was carrying ten million passengers a year. Woodside station opened in 1878, and it was curiously designed, for whilst its main entrance faced the river, its passengers used a 'temporary' doorway on one side.

Through trains to Paddington were a great feature of the station and survived until 1967, in which year the station closed. In the 'past' view, Stanier '5MT' No. 45004 awaits departure with the 1145am to Paddington on September 17 1966. In 1988, little remained to recall the railway's presence. Part of the site was serving as a car park whilst part was derelict. However, on March 23 1988 surveyors were at work at Woodside, probably gathering data required to plan redevelopment for this historic site. *Neville Knight/JCH.*

TITLE PAGE:
NORTHWICH: On August 20 1955, LNER Class D11/1 4-4-0 No. 62661 *Gerard Powys Dewhurst* is in charge of the 12.52pm Chester Northgate-Manchester Central service at Northwich. On the left, Ivatt '2MT' 2-6-2T No. 41229 has arrived with the 12.38pm from Crewe. This is a scene rich in the atmosphere of the BR steam years. By 1988, all locomotive-hauled trains between Chester and Manchester had been taken over by DMUs, with Class 142 *Pacers* making an occasional appearance. The passenger service to Crewe ended in 1960, although the line remains open for freight traffic. The 'present' picture shows Northwich on August 16 1987, as Class 142 No. 142-068 awaits departure with the 1008 Chester-Manchester Piccadilly service. In the intervening years the canopies have been either demolished, or cut back and repainted, whilst the elegant gas lighting equipment has given way to more modern electric lamps. The tall, lower quadrant semaphores have passed into history along with the greasetop caps seen being worn by the railwaymen in the old picture. *Brian Morrison/JCH.*

BIBLIOGRAPHY

A Regional History of the Railways of Great Britain:
  Vol 7 - The West Midlands *by Rex Christiansen (David & Charles).*
  Vol 10 - The North West *by Geoffrey O. Holt (David & Charles).*
  Vol 11 - North & Mid Wales *by Peter E. Baughan (David & Charles).*
Complete British Railways Maps & Gazetteer from 1830-1981 *(OPC).*
An Historical Survey of the Chester & Holyhead Railway *by V.R. Anderson & G.K. Fox (OPC).*
An Illustrated History of the Cheshire Lines Committe *by Paul Bolger (Heyday).*
Railways of the Macclesfield District *by Basil Jeuda (Wyvern).*
Forgotten Railways - North & Mid Wales *by Rex Christiansen (David & Charles).*

© Silver Link Publishing Ltd/Paul Shannon and John Hillmer

All rights reserved. No part of this publication may be reproduced, stored in a retrieval system or transmitted, in any form or by any means, electronic, mechanical, photocopying, recording or otherwise, without prior permission in writing from Past & Present Publishing Ltd.

First published in November 1988
Reprinted May 1993

Printed and bound in Great Britain

British Library Cataloguing in Publication Data

British Railways Past and Present
Vol 6: Cheshire & North Wales
  1. Railroads–Great Britain–History
  I. Shannon, Paul. II. Hillmer, John
385'.0941 HE3018

ISBN 1 85895 008 2

Past & Present Publishing Ltd
Unit 5, Home Farm Close
Church Street, Wadenhoe
Peterborough PE8 5TE
Tel/fax (08015) 4-4-0

CUDDINGTON: This station is located on the former Cheshire Lines Committee route between Northwich and Chester. Opened to passenger traffic in 1870, it was the junction for the branch to Winsford & Over, which had a rather chequered history until it finally closed to passenger traffic in 1931. In the 'past' view (top), LNER Class 04 2-8-0 No. 63661 is heading west with a mixed freight, in May 1954. The modern view shows the same location on May 22 1988, as a two car Class 108 DMU approaches the station, forming the 1633 Manchester Piccadilly-Chester service. The station still serves a rural community but is closed on Sundays today. The signal box and its signals have gone, together with the crossover, single slip sidings, small goods shed and platform benches, which carry the station name. Note how the station has become enclosed by trees. This is commonly found at many locations and can make the railway photographer's hobby very difficult! *N. R. Knight/JCH.*

INTRODUCTION

As will be seen from the map on the inside front cover of this book, the railway network of Cheshire & North Wales was once very intricate, considering how sparsely populated most of the area was – and indeed, still is today. To some extent this was a reflection of the competition between rival Companies of the pre-Grouping era, although the actual duplication of routes and terminal stations is largely limited to the north eastern fringe of our area.

This is not intended to be a history book, but it is nevertheless appropriate here to briefly review the pattern of growth and decline in the area's railways. Both in Cheshire and in North Wales, the Great Western Railway had a strong presence, with its trunk route to Birkenhead passing through Shrewsbury, Wrexham and Chester, as well as the former Cambrian lines linking Shropshire with the Welsh Coast. More significant, however, at least as far as longer distance traffic is concerned, was the London & North Western Railway, bisecting Cheshire with its main line from London to Scotland and reaching westwards as far as Holyhead. The town of Crewe owes its existence to the LMS and its forebears, having become established in the earliest days both as an important junction and interchange point for passenger and goods traffic and as a centre for the construction and maintenance of locomotives. These functions are still performed by Crewe in 1988, with the exception of freight marshalling, which has been transferred to Warrington.

Mention also needs to be made of the London & North Eastern Railway, whose interests (inherited from the Great Central Railway) extended to western parts with its involvement in the Cheshire Lines Committee as well as its own line from Bidston to Wrexham. One interesting result of all this was that locomotives from three of the four pre-Nationalisation companies could once be seen in Wrexham and Chester.

Decline was already under way in the 1930s, with the lines to Red Wharf Bay (Anglesey), Dyserth and Winsford & Over all losing their passenger services at an early date. More branches succumbed during the 1950s, leaving places like Holywell, St Asaph and Bethesda devoid of passenger railway connection. And, after Dr Beeching's Report appeared in 1963, many more routes were destined to face the axe, such as Bangor to Afon Wen, Ruabon to Bala, Nantwich to Wellington and the old GWR terminus at Birkenhead Woodside.

Not all is on the debit side, however. The sadness which accompanies visits to towns such as Leek, Market Drayton, Caernarfon and Ruthin, to name but a few casualties of railway cutbacks, is tempered by the vibrancy of the surviving system. The benefits of increased investment by BR are becoming apparent, with station re-openings such as Conwy and Valley, the widespread introduction of *Sprinter* trains, the major remodelling of Crewe's track layout in 1985 to allow through trains to pass at high speed for the first time, and even the re-opening of a freight-only line from Dee Marsh to Mickle Trafford. Passenger traffic has been given a boost on the Cambrian lines with the reintroduction of locomotive-hauled trains to Barmouth and Pwllheli, as well as with the *Sprinter* units already mentioned.

Prospects for freight traffic are generally bright, too, especially around Deeside. Recent years have witnessed the renewal of a major contract with Associated Octel for moving chemicals to and from Amlwch, the opening of new facilities for the Shotton Paper Company for timber (in) and newsprint (out) and the establishment of the Cawoods coal container terminal at Ellesmere Port, supplied by regular company trains from South Wales and the North East. All this gives us cause for optimism for the railways of Cheshire & North Wales.

In conclusion, we offer our sincere thanks to the many photographers who have allowed us to make use of their material, together with the railwaymen and enthusiasts who have shared their knowledge with us in providing accurate caption details, and helping to locate some of the more elusive vantage points featured in these pages.

Paul Shannon & John Hillmer,
Summer 1988

RHAGYMADRODD

Fel y gwelir ar y map atodedig, bu rhwyd-waith rheilffyrdd Swydd Gaer a Gogledd Cymru, ar un cyfnod, yn un cymhleth iawn, o ystyried mor denau yr oedd (ac y mae) poblogaeth y rhan fwyaf o'r rhanbarth. I raddau, yr oedd y cymhlethdod hwn yn adlewyrchiad o'r cystadlu a fodolai rhwng cwmniau rheilffyrdd y cyfnod cyn y Grwpio - er bod dyblygu ar wasanaethau a therfynfeydd yn gyfyngedig, gan fwyaf, at ymylon gogledd-ddwyreiniol yr ardal sydd dan sylw.

Nid llyfr hanes mo'r gyfrol hon, ond priodol yw bwrw golwg byr dros y patrwm o dyfiant ac edwino a welwyd ar reilffyrdd yr ardal. Bu gan gwmni'r Great Western rwyd-waith sylweddol yn Swydd Gaer a Gogledd Cymru fel ei gilydd, gyda'i brif reilffordd i Benbedw yn rhedeg drwy'r Amwythig, Wrecsam a Chaer, a chledrau hen gwmni'r Cambrian yn cysylltu Sir Amwythig ag arfordir Bae Ceredigion. Pwysicach, fodd bynnag - o leiaf lle'r oedd trafnidiaeth taith-hirach yn y cwestiwn - oedd Rheilffordd y London & North Western, a rychwantai Swydd Gaer gyda'i brif lein o Lundain i'r Alban, ac a ymestynnai i'r gorllewin cyn belled â Chaergybi. Y mae tref Crewe yn ddyledus i gwmni'r LMS a'i ragflaenwyr am ei bodolaeth: fe'i sefydlwyd yn nyddiau cyn-haraf y rheilffyrdd fel cyffordd pwysig ac fel man ymgyfnewid i drafnidiaeth teithwyr a nwyddau, a hefyd fel canolfan adeiladu a chynnal-a-chadw ar gyfer injans. Diddorol yw sylwi bod hyn i gyd yn parhau i ddig-wydd yng Nghrewe heddiw, ac eithrio'r gwaith o farsialu trenau nwyddau, a gyflawnir bellach yn Warrington.

Dylid cofio hefyd am gwmni'r London & North Eastern, a oedd wedi etifeddu, oddi wrth hen gwmni'r Great Central, ran yng ngweithgaredd y 'Cheshire Lines Committee,' yn ogystal â'r lein o Fidston i Wrecsam. Un canlyniad diddorol oedd bod modd gweld yng Nghaer a Wrecsam, ar un cyfnod, injans o eiddo tri o'r pedwar cwmni mawr a fodolai cyn Gwladoliad 1948.

Fodd bynnag, yr oedd dirywiad eisoes ar droed erbyn y 1930au, gyda'r rheilffyrdd i Draeth Coch, Dyserth a Winsford & Over i gyd yn colli eu gwasanaethau i deithwyr yn y cyfnod hwnnw. Collwyd rhagor o wasanaethau yn y 1950au, gan adael cymdo-gaethau fel Treffynnon, Llanelwy a Bethesda heb drenau ar gyfer teithwyr. Ac wedi Adroddiad Beeching ym 1963, syrthiodd rhagor dan y fwyell, gan gynnwys y gwasanaethau o Fangor i Afon Wen, o Riwabon i'r Bala, ac o Nantwich i Wellington, a hefyd hen derfynfa'r GWR yn Woodside, Penbedw.

Sut bynnag, nid du mo'r llun i gyd. Lleddfir rhyw gymaint ar y tristwch a ddaw wrth ymweld â threfi fel Leek, Market Drayton, Caernarfon a'r Rhuthun - i enwi dim ond ychydig o'r rhai a amddifadwyd yn sgîl y toriadau yn y rhwydwaith rheilffyrdd - gan fywiogrwydd yr hyn sy'n weddill. Bellach, gwelir canlyniadau'r cynnydd a fu mewn buddsoddi gan y Rheilffyrdd Prydeinig, gydag ail-agor gorsafoedd yng Nghonwy a'r Fali; dyfodiad y trenau 'Sprinter'; adlunio cynllun y cledrau yng Nghrewe ym 1985 er mwyn galluogi i rai trenau basio drwy'r orsaf ar gyflymdra uchel am y tro cyntaf; a hyd yn oed ail-agor y lein o Wern Dyfrdwy i Mickle Trafford ar gyfer trenau nwyddau. Atgyfnerthwyd y gwasanaeth i deithwyr ar leiniau'r Cambrian gan ddychweliad trenau injan-a-cherbydau i'r Bermo a Phwllheli, yn ychwanegol at y trenau 'Sprinter' a grybwyllwyd eisoes.

Mae'r rhagolygon ar gyfer trafnidiaeth nwyddau, hefyd, yn obeithiol at ei gilydd, yn enwedig yn ardal y gororau o gwmpas Glannau Dyfrdwy. Yn ystod y blynyddoedd diweddar, gwelwyd adnewyddu'r cytundeb pwysig gyda Chwmni Associated Octel i gludo cemegolion rhwng Amlwch ac Ellesmere Port; sefydlwyd cyfleusterau newydd er mwyn galluogi Cwmni Papur Shotton i fewngludo coedwydd ac allgludo papur ar gyfer papurau newydd; a sefydlwyd terfynell amlwythi-glo cwmni Cawoods yn Ellesmere Port, sy'n derbyn trenau-cwmni rheolaidd o Dde Cymru a Gogledd-Ddwyrain Lloegr. Mae hyn oll yn argoeli'n galonogol ar gyfer dyfodol y rhwydwaith rheilffyrdd yn Swydd Gaer a Gogledd Cymru.

I gloi, hoffem ddiolch yn ddiffuant iawn i'r ffotograffwyr niferus hynny a ganiatâodd i ni wneud defnydd o'u gwaith, ynghyd â'r holl weithwyr a chefnogwyr rheilffyrdd a

rannodd eu gwybodaeth â ni wrth ddarparu manylion cywir ar gyfer y nodiadau disgrifiadol, ac wrth gynnig cymorth i ni ddarganfod rhai o'r golygfannau llai adnabyddus a ddefnyddiwyd i dynnu rhai o'r lluniau a gynhwysir yn y tudalennau sy'n dilyn.

Paul Shannon a John Hillmer,
Haf 1988
(Cyfieithiad: Wyn Hobson)

BANGOR (EAST END) : Tightly positioned between two tunnels, Bangor is the last major station before Holyhead on the North Wales coastal main line. It had its own goods yard and locomotive depot, whilst the station had two through lines accompanied by Up and Down loops, and bay platforms. Our 'past' view shows a rare visit to Bangor by Riddles '4MT' No. 76040 on April 16 1966, in charge of a Down parcels train. A Metro-Cammell DMU is stabled on the right in the former Bethesda branch bay. *Wyn Hobson/PDS.*

NORTH EAST CHESHIRE

WILMSLOW has a railway history dating from 1842, when the Manchester & Birmingham Railway was opened as far as Sandbach. Later the same year, the line was extended to Crewe, where it joined the Grand Junction Railway, to become part of the LNWR. Wilmslow gained junction status when the Styal Loop was opened in 1909. Electrification was completed in 1961 and a Power Box opened. Above: LMS rebuilt 'Royal Scot' 4-6-0 No. 46162 *Queens Westminster Rifleman* (allocated to 1B, Camden) crosses the River Bollin as it slows for the stop, with the morning Manchester London Road (now Piccadilly)-West of England express, in 1957. When the line was electrified, the platforms were extended, as illustrated in the 'present' view (right) and the semaphores replaced by colour light signals. Sprinter No 150 208 is pictured entering the station with a Manchester-Cardiff service on May 30 1988. *Martin Welch/JCH.*

SANDBACH: A short North Staffordshire line, which left the Manchester-Crewe main line just south of Sandbach, ran to Alsager where it joined the Crewe-Kidsgrove route. It was authorised by Act of Parliament in 1846 amongst several lines promoted by the NSR at the same time. Passenger traffic survived until 1930, when the region suffered the effects of industrial depression, although the line remained open for freight until 1971. Above: Horwich-built 'Crab' 2-6-0 No 42727 is pictured near Sandbach on April 23 1966, heading towards Alsager, with an RCTS rail tour. The modern picture, taken on September 12 1987, presents a sad sight: the railway has been completely obliterated. *Michael Mensing/JCH.*

MACCLESFIELD locomotive depot was close to the town's Hibel Road station and provided power primarily for local trains to Manchester. It was coded 9C(a sub-shed of Longsight) and in the 1950s had an allocation of a dozen or so engines, mainly LMS 2-6-4Ts. The evocative 'past' picture taken around 1958, shows Fowler 2-6-4T No 42318 and Stanier 2-6-4T No 42443 being prepared for their day's work. The site was cleared completely following closure, as seen on April 4 1988. Subsequent development prevented an identical viewpoint, but the contrast is poignant nevertheless.
Martin Welch/JCH.

MACCLESFIELD CENTRAL (1): On a summer Saturday in 1956 (above) 'Patriot' 4-6-0- No 45501 *St Dunstans* storms through Macclesfield Central Station with an Up Relief to the 'Pines Express'. On the left, LMS 2-6-4T No 42363 waits for a clear road, with a Down freight. *Martin Welch.*

Above: Class 47 No 47450 is approaching the station with the 1030 Manchester Piccadilly-Euston service on Sunday, January 10 1988. Remodelling of the station resulted in the demolition of the signalbox, which was replaced by a modern structure on the opposite side of the line. The mill in the background remains much the same, apart from the alteration to the top of the tower. *JCH.*

MACCLESFIELD CENTRAL (2): Pictured circa 1953 (above) BR 'Britannia' 4-6-2 No 70033 *Charles Dickens* passes Macclesfield Central with the 2.05pm Manchester London Road (now Piccadilly) to Euston, with banking assistance. This station has been remodelled and only the building with the pointed roof (visible beneath the gantry in the old view) survives to positively locate the new picture. The old LNWR station at Hibel Road, closed in 1960 when services were concentrated at Central.
Martin Welch/JCH.

PRESTBURY lies a few miles north of Macclesfield, on the main line from Manchester to Stafford (via Stoke-on-Trent), its origins dating from 1845. The village it serves is a Cheshire 'showpiece' attracting many visitors. Above: On March 27 1959, LMS 'Black 5' 4-6-0 No. 45109 passes the station with the 1.55pm Manchester London Road (now Piccadilly)-Euston express. *Michael Mensing.*

Below: The same viewpoint today, and there has been much change in character. Electrification of the line was accompanied by demolition of the signal box, and the sidings have gone, but the station building survives. On April 4 1988, Class 47 No. 47481 passes with the 1401 to Stafford. *JCH.*

BOLLINGTON is just north of Macclesfield, and was served by the line linking Marple Wharf Junction with Macclesfield Central, which had its origins in the 1864 incorporation of the Macclesfield Bollington & Marple Railway. The station handled considerable goods traffic for the local textile industry, principally raw cotton from Liverpool, also coal. During January 1970 (above) a local train is approaching the station in the last days of service. Following closure, the trackbed became a footpath now known as the Middlewood Way, as seen in the modern view.
Martin Welch/JCH.

NORTH STAFFORDSHIRE

RUSHTON: This tidy station was located in delightful country on the North Staffordshire Railway's Churnet Valley line between North Rode and Uttoxeter, opened in 1849. Regular passenger services ceased in 1960, goods being withdrawn in 1964. Relations between the NSR and the LNWR were often strained, but the 'Knotty' remained independent until absorption into the LMS in 1923. The old picture shows Fowler 2-6-4T No. 42421 leaving the station on September 30 1959, with the 12.57pm Macclesfield- (Hibel Road)-Uttoxeter service. *Michael Mensing.*

Below: The much-changed modern view, of May 1988. The platforms now form part of the garden attached to the old station house. *JCH.*

LEEK: With origins dating back to 1849 and formerly a through station on the Churnet Valley line, Leek became a terminus in 1960 with the closure to passengers of the link with the Stoke-Manchester line, at North Rode. The station survived for a further five years before the town lost is passenger railway entirely. Stanier 2-6-4T No. 42454 is pictured (above) on August 20 1962, in charge of the 4.30pm train to Uttoxeter. *Ian Holt.*

Right: With the exception of the roadbridge, all trace of the railway at Leek has been swept away. The station site is pictured in light industrial use on September 6 1987. *JCH.*

ALTON TOWERS : Completed in 1849, the Churnet Valley line, between North Rode and Uttoxeter, was one of the North Staffordshire Railway's more scenic routes, far removed in character from the dense network of lines in the industrial Potteries. Regular passenger trains were withdrawn from the Churnet Valley line in 1960, although workmen's trains between Leek and Uttoxeter persisted for a further five years. One such train, the 11.18 am Uttoxeter-Leek service, is pictured (above) arriving at Alton Towers station on August 19 1961, headed by Stanier 2-6-4T No. 42667. *Michael Mensing.*

Above: The Churnet Valley line was closed completely south of Oakamoor in 1965, but Alton Towers station has been kept alive as a private house (see also page 2) and the platforms and access steps from the road overbridge still remain in situ. This view is dated April 13 1988. Just a few miles to the north, the railway was still in daily use, at the time of going to press, conveying block loads of sand from Oakamoor to St Helens, in Lancashire. *PDS.*

CHEADLE was not connected to the railway network until 1901, for the branch passed over awkward terrain and ran into trouble soon after its authorisation in 1888. The tunnel that was eventually built on the line continued to cause problems and the LMS built a diversionary route to avoid the offending hill altogether in 1933. Sand and gravel traffic kept the branch open for freight until recent times (the official closure date was May 12 1986), but passenger services had ceased 23 years earlier, in June 1963. The single-platform terminus at Cheadle is pictured during the last month of operation, on June 4 1963, with Stanier 2-6-4T No. 42665 ready to depart with the 5.35pm service to Stoke-on-Trent. *John Marshall.*

Above: The deserted station, devoid of all buildings, on April 13 1988. The rails are rusted over, though still usable. *PDS.*

HANLEY: Like the Cheadle branch, the North Staffordshire Railway's loop line from Stoke to Kidsgrove via Hanley and Burslem was a comparatively late arrival on the scene. It was completed on November 15 1875, ten years after its authorisation. It gave access to a number of collieries, in addition to its role as a heavily used passenger line. Hanley station is pictured (above) on September 28 1963, with a three-car DMU forming the 1.55 pm Macclesfield-Stoke-on-Trent service. *Michael Mensing.*

Left: Little remains of the railway today. The cutting has been filled, but one of the original road overbridge parapets survives. The building on the right is still recognisable, although it has lost its chimneys. April 13 1987. *PDS.*

BURSLEM: The 4.19 pm service from Uttoxeter to Congleton approaches Burslem station (above) on September 28 1963, formed by a Birmingham RC&W three-car DMU. Loop line services via Hanley and Burslem were a casualty of the Beeching era, ceasing altogether on March 2 1964. *Michael Mensing.*

Above: The same location on April 13 1988, showing the recreational walkway created by the City of Stoke on this section of the closed line. The overbridge has been removed and infilled, around a small pedestrian-sized opening. *PDS.*

NEWCHAPEL & GOLDENHILL also lay on the Potteries loop line, and despite the apparently rural setting was surrounded by collieries and opencast workings, the last of which survived into the 1970s. Above: a six-car DMU formation is seen rolling into Newchapel on September 28 1963, working the 4.18pm Macclesfield-Wolverhampton High Level service. *Michael Mensing.*

Below: The iron railings and platform edge serve to positively identify the location on April 13 1988, as horse-riders and walkers make use of the overgrown trackbed. *PDS.*

KIDSGROVE LIVERPOOL ROAD: Our last photograph featuring the 'loop' line dates from 1960, when steam-hauled passenger trains were still much in evidence. Above: On September 26 of that year, Stanier 2-6-4T No. 42668 arrives at Liverpool Road station with empty stock from Crewe, which will form an evening workers' train back to the Royal Ordnance Factory at Radway Green. The station closed in 1964. An unusual operating practice at Kidsgrove was the reversing of trains between Crewe line and 'loop' line junctions, so that two cumbersome run-round movements could be avoided. No. 42668 would therefore have propelled its stock up the line from Kidsgrove Central before entering Liverpool Road station 'locomotive first' as pictured here. *Michael Mensing.*

Below: By April 1988, willows and birches had taken over much of the station area at Kidsgrove Liverpool Road, leaving only the platform edges as indications of its past. In the background are the masts and gantries of the surviving electrified line from Stoke to Macclesfield. *PDS.*

KIDSGROVE CENTRAL is the junction where the line from Crewe joins the Manchester Piccadilly-Stafford main line. Above: LMS 'Jinty' 0-6-0T No. 47596 reverses its short freight along the Up main line towards Stoke, to gain access to the Crewe line, on September 26 1960. *Michael Mensing.*

Left: The same scene on November 14 1987 as 'Sprinter' No. 150 137 approaches with the 0942 Boston (Lincs)-Crewe service. Following electrification of the Manchester line, the signal box was demolished and a new structure built on the opposite side of the junction. *JCH.*

WHEELOCK was the first station from Sandbach on the North Staffordshire Railway line to Kidsgrove, which left the LNWR main line between Manchester and Crewe at Wheelock Junction. The original line from Lawton Junction to Wheelock opened to goods in 1852 and to passenger traffic in 1893. In 1930, passenger services ceased but freight continued until 1956. The old picture shows a joint SLS/MLS charter train, shortly before closure. Today, the railway serves as a walkway, and whilst the trees now obscure the road bridge the platform is carefully preserved. *Neville Knight/JCH.*

HARECASTLE TUNNEL (1): The railway north from Stoke to Harecastle was opened in the summer of 1849, to connect with the Harecastle-Congleton section which had been completed in the previous year. At Harecastle, three tunnels needed to be constructed, and BR Class 5 4-6-0 No. 73014 is pictured (below) emerging from the southernmost bore with an Up mineral train on June 4 1963. *John Marshall.*

Left: The Harecastle tunnels proved a major obstacle during electrification of the Stoke-Macclesfield main line in the 1960s, and a 2 1/2-mile deviation was built to the west. It was opened on June 27 1966, when the original route was closed. The deserted southern portal of the main old tunnel is pictured on April 13 1988. *PDS.*

HARECASTLE TUNNEL (2) : The new trackwork at the southern end of the Harecastle deviation was already in place, though not yet commissioned, when this view (below) of a DMU local service from Stoke-on-Trent was taken on March 5 1966. *John Marshall.*

Above: Part of the original alignment was used for storage sidings after closure as a through route, and those sidings can still be seen on the left. On April 13 1987, Class 47 locomotive No. 47283 is heading for Crewe diesel depot after working a freight train to Longport. *PDS.*

SILVERDALE: One rather depressing aspect of compiling a book such as this is that many of the 'past' photographs depict a busy, healthy railway whereas most of the 'present' pictures show a reduction of facilities, or even complete abandonment and redevelopment. At Silverdale, there is a happier story to tell, for despite the loss of passenger services the location remains busy with merry-go-round coal trains from Silverdale Colliery to Ironbridge Power Station, plus (less frequent) trainloads of coal from Holditch Colliery to Llanwern. In the 'present' photograph, taken on April 13 1988, Class 20s Nos. 20005 and 20032 pass alongside Silverdale's former Down platform whilst running round their train of empty HAAs. Less than an hour later, the loaded train will be heading for Ironbridge. A new rapid loading bunker has been erected over the former Up line, with the Down line slewed to the left to maintain clearances. Silverdale's origins go back to the days of the North Staffordshire Railway, when it formed part of their line from Stoke to Market Drayton. This was closed as a through route to passengers in 1956 and to freight ten years later, but the section from Apedale Junction to Madeley (where a new connection to the West Coast Main Line had been made in 1962) was retained. At the eastern end of the line, a 'shuttle' service of DMUs between Stoke, Newcastle and Silverdale continued in operation until 1964, and our 'past' picture shows a Birmingham RCW two-car unit employed on this service on August 20 1962.
Ian Holt/PDS.

WEST COAST MAIN LINE & CREWE

ACTON GRANGE JUNCTION lies on the WCML immediately south of the Manchester Ship Canal bridge, which itself marks the southern end of Warrington's extensive freight yards. Above : An English Electric Type 4 (later Class 40) is seen approaching Acton Grange with an Up parcels train in the late 1960s , whilst Type 2 locomotives Nos. D5008 and D5019 head north on the main line towards Warrington. *Keith Sanders.*

Above: Class 87 No. 87030 *Black Douglas* passes the same point whilst working the Up 'Royal Scot' (0845 Ayr - Euston) of October 17 1987. A maze of wires and masts has replaced the semaphore signals of the earlier picture, creating a completely different atmosphere, though the trackwork remains essentially the same. *PDS.*

MOORE is a few miles south of Warrington on the WCML and once boasted a station, which closed in 1943. As seen in the old photograph of BR 4-6-2 'Britannia' No. 70053 *Moray Firth*, there were also water troughs, accompanied by a water tower (on the skyline). The Pacific is steaming south with a mixed freight, on a summer evening in 1966 throwing up a lot of spray as the tender scoop collects water. The tower has gone and the trees have grown considerably in the intervening 22 year span. *Keith Sanders.*

Left: Class 87 No. 87007 *City of Manchester* is pictured on May 5 1988, with the 1410 Glasgow-Euston service. *JCH.*

CREWE is probably the most famous station in the world. Undoubtedly, the railway created the town, for when the Grand Junction Railway opened in 1837, the tiny hamlet of Crewe had a population of just 184 souls. Locomotive building began in 1845 and continues to this day. The London & North Western Railway, known as 'The Premier Line', was of enormous significance. By 1903 the Company employed more than 10,000 people at Crewe. At the heart of the WCML between Euston and Glasgow, Crewe is the junction of lines from Chester (and thus North Wales), Manchester, Stoke and Shrewsbury. The GWR gained a foothold (with even a small locomotive shed) and the NSR too, with exchange sidings and a goods depot. There were two large loco sheds in steam days, one at the north end (long disappeared) and one at the south end (which remains). Generally speaking, North Shed catered for passenger work and South Shed for freight. 1961 witnessed completion of the first section of electrification between Manchester and Crewe, followed by the Liverpool section in 1962. In 1985, the station was extensively remodelled, resulting in virtual closure of the station for a period, one of the subsequent benefits being much faster through running of trains.

CREWE (1) : Major rationalisation at Crewe in 1985 included the removal of track from the two Down bays at the north end of the station. In the November 26 1960 picture LMS 'Jubilee' No. 45571 *South Africa* (carrying a 24E shedplate - Blackpool) is in charge of the 12.15pm to Blackpool Central, standing alongside brand new Type 4 (Class 40) No D216, with the 12.08pm to Bangor. *Michael Mensing.*

Right: This September 2 1987 view shows how passenger services have virtually ceased on this side of the station, with through platform No. 12 only used for stopping trains in unusual circumstances. *JCH.*

CREWE (2) : On September 19 1961, GWR 'Manor' 4-6-0 No.7809 *Childrey Manor* stands in one of the bays at the south end of Crewe station. GWR locomotives worked regularly into Crewe and the Company had a small engine shed at Gresty Lane (a sub-shed of Wellington), closed in 1963. This scene has changed very little and the latter-day views shows a DMU with the 1416 service to Llandovery, on October 28 1987. Normally, this train would have run through to Swansea but due to severe flooding, the bridge collapsed over the River Tywi on October 19 1987, as a Swansea-Shrewsbury train started to cross it, resulting in the tragic drowning of the driver and three passengers. *Michael Mensing/JCH.*

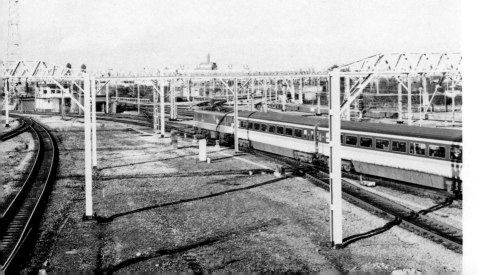

CREWE (3): Above: Passing through the station on July 27 1955 is 'Black 5' 4-6-0 No. 45446, with a down troop train from the Southern Region. The Chester line diverges to the left, the WCML heads straight ahead whilst the Manchester line curves off to the right. *Brian Morrison.*

Left: A similar view on October 28 1987, as No. 86414 *Frank Hornby* leaves with a Euston-Blackpool North service. Crewe North Junction signalbox is now part of the Heritage Centre. *JCH.*

AROUND NORTHWICH

NORTHWICH SHED (1) : LNER Class 04 2-8-0 No.63743 stands in front of the shed at Northwich in 1960. Being a former CLC depot, there were always LNER locos to be seen, including 4-4-0 'Directors' and 'J10' 0-6-0s, as well as LMS engines, particularly '8F' 2-8-0s, which were the mainstay on the limestone trains from Buxton to the ICI Works at Northwich. The building remains intact in 1988, but all track was lifted following closure.
Hugh Ballantyne/JCH.

NORTHWICH SHED (2) : A few 'D6' and 'D9' 4-4-0s, 'L3' 2-6-4Ts and 'N5' 0-6-2Ts were also allocated to Northwich, for passenger work. A good selection of LNER engines can be seen in this 'past' photograph, taken around 1960, with 'J10' No.65158 in the foreground whilst No 65169 is being coaled. A powerful 'A4' 4-6-2T (used for banking) is visible beyond the turntable. Closed to steam in 1968, the shed remained in use for diesels well into the 1980s. The latter-day view of May 15 1988 shows the four-lane shed building intact, although all track has been removed. At the time of going to press, this was the only former CLC shed still standing. *Neville Knight/JCH.*

NORTHWICH: Approaching Northwich station on August 8 1955 (above) is LNER Class 04/7 2-8-0 No. 63794, with a westbound freight. Once a bustling area for goods traffic, Northwich is much quieter these days, although there are still (at the time of going to press) three trains daily from Buxton, carrying limestone to the ICI works at Northwich, as well as regular cement and oil trains. *Brian Morrison.*

Above: A similar view on August 16 1987. The semaphores have all gone and the track has been rationalised, as Class 37s Nos. 37688 and 37687 shunt hopper wagons in the ICI yard. *JCH.*

WINSFORD & OVER station was at the end of a short branch which left the Northwich-Chester line just west of Cuddington. Opened in 1870, this CLC line had one intermediate station, at Whitegate, and a short spur ran to a salt works at Winsford, from Falks Junction. The line had a chequered history with passenger services ceasing in 1874, re-starting in 1886, withdrawn again in 1888, recommenced in 1892 before finally ceasing in 1931! It remained open for goods until 1958.   Top:

LNER 'C13' 4-4-2T No.67436 at Winsford on the occasion of an RCTS tour in 1953 - note the Clerestory coach. *Neville Knight.*

Above: Today, the station area at Winsford & Over has been swallowed by a modern road system, although the wooden shed on the extreme left still stands, behind the trees shown in the modern picture, taken on July 3 1988. *JCH.*

FRODSHAM: In July 1946 (above) LNWR 'G1' 0-8-0 No. 8924 passes through Frodsham (between Chester and Warrington), with an eastbound freight. Nothing remains of the signalbox, and all sidings have been removed, although the station building has changed little, other than the loss of the platform canopy. The line is still reasonably busy with passenger traffic from North Wales to Manchester and beyond, but there are no locomotive-hauled passenger trains, most services being operated by Sprinters. A variety of freight continues, including oil and chemicals from Ellesmere Port, daily *Freightliner* workings between Holyhead and Trafford Park (Manchester), and, as seen in the modern picture, steel coil is carried between Mossend and the John Summers Steel Works at Dee Marsh. On June 20 1987, Class 20s Nos. 20161 and 20040 are in charge of empty steel coil flats comprising 6S42, the 0917 from Dee Marsh Junction. *Frank Dean/JCH.*

HELSBY is the junction of the Wirral line (from Birkenhead) with the main line from Warrington to Chester. Above: An early-liveried DMU is awaiting departure with the 3.08pm to Birkenhead Woodside. Although the latter station was closed in 1967, the service continues to the present day with trains terminating at Hooton. The station has changed very little other than the loss of the footbridge roof. The modern picture was taken on June 27 1987 and shows a Hooton train formed of two Class 108 DMUs.
Ian G Holt/JCH.

CHESTER (1). Stanier Class 5MT 4-6-0 No 45091 arrives at Chester from Manchester in the early 1960s, with two sister engines standing in the background. The mass of lower quadrant semaphores, together with the imposing LNWR signal box, have all gone, replaced by colour lights. Some track simplification has also taken place, as shown in the modern picture of August 20 1987, with Class 47 No.47298 standing on the left with the Llandudno Junction to Walton Old Junction Speedlink. *Tom Heavyside/JCH.*

CHESTER (2) : On February 1 1964, Stanier '8F' 2-8-0 No. 48259 trundles through with a westbound train of oil tanks. It carries a 6B shed plate (Mold Junction). *Ian Holt.*

Below: The same scene on August 20 1987, as Class 47 No.47432 arrives with a Euston-Holyhead train. The scissors crossover, once a common feature at major stations, has been replaced by a simple crossover, whilst only a hole in the wall recalls the signal cabin. *JCH.*

CHESTER NORTHGATE: The Cheshire Lines Committee was formed in 1865, with the Manchester, Sheffield & Lincolnshire Railway and Great Northern as joint owners, with the Midland Railway becoming a partner the following year. Chester Northgate was opened in 1875, with principal services to Manchester Central (via Northwich) and to Wrexham Exchange and Central. It was a four-road station with two platform faces. Nearby was a small engine shed which in 1947 had an allocation of a dozen LNER engines. It closed in 1960 and the station followed in 1969 and traffic was transferred to Chester General.

Above: On August 20 1955, 'D11/1' No.62661 *Gerard Powys Dewhurst* is heading a train for Manchester Central. Left: The whole site has been re-developed as a the Northgate Arena sports complex; all trace of the railway has been eradicated. *Brian Morrison/JCH.*

BROXTON: The short line from Waverton (on the Chester-Crewe route) ran through a delightful rural landscape to Whitchurch and survived until 1957. Above: LMS 2-6-4T No. 42594, then allocated to Longsight shed, pauses with an Up train, early in 1958. An attractive view of a typical country station. *Neville Knight.*

Right: Since closure, the railway has been completely erased from the landscape, and the station site now serves as a picnic area. Probably few of the motorists who park here to eat their sandwiches even know the previous history of the site. *JCH.*

GREEN LANE CROSSING : Class 8F 2-8-0 No. 48255, with an Up oil train, approaches the level crossing near Saltney on February 1 1964. This location is on the GWR main line between Chester and Wrexham. *Ian Holt.*

Above: Saltney Sidings have disappeared completely, and bushes and trees have taken over where once lines of wagons could be found. Also, the double track main line has been reduced to single track. On September 4 1987, Class 47 No. 47318 is heading the 0625 *Speedlink* service from Warrington Arpley to Shotton Paper Company. The train runs to Croes Newydd North Fork (Wrexham) where the locomotive runs round and then takes the Wrexham-Bidston line to its destination. *JCH.*

THE WIRRAL

HOOTON is unusual in that although effectively a 'through' station, all passenger services terminate! This was by no means always so, as the origins of the line began with the Chester & Birkenhead Railway in 1840 with through services. The line to Helsby opened in 1863, followed in 1866 with the branch to Parkgate, on the west side of the peninsula, ultimately extended to West Kirby. Today, third-rail EMUs link Liverpool and Hooton, where passengers change to continue their journey by DMU, either to Chester or Helsby. Of the six platforms, only three are in regular use.

Above: In the 'past' picture, GWR '5101' Class 2-6-2T No.5176 is seen with a branch line train to West Kirby on August 7 1954. The modern picture (right) shows Class 508 No. 508 115, on March 23 1988, with a Liverpool train. *Neville Knight/JCH.*

44

ROCK FERRY lies a few miles south of Birkenhead on the line to Chester. The original station, named Rock Lane, opened in 1846, but this closed in 1862 and was replaced by Rock Ferry, slightly further north. In 1860, the line was taken over jointly by the GWR and LNWR giving the former Company access to Birkenhead, and via the Ferry over to Liverpool.

The Mersey Railway opened in 1891 and by 1898 there was a through service from Liverpool Central (Low Level) to Paddington via the junction at Rock Ferry. There has since been considerable rationalisation of track, as shown on March 23 1988. *N.R. Knight.*

Above: LMS 2-6-4T No.42647 enters the station with the 2.45pm Birkenhead-Paddington service, which would be re-engined at Chester, during 1966, on a line which has subsequently been lifted. Apart from the electric commuter service, the remaining track is used only by a small number of freight trains carrying traffic to and from Birkenhead Docks.*JCH.*

BIRKENHEAD NORTH is east of the junction at which the metals from New Brighton join the line from West Kirby. The first Wirral Railway Company was incorporated in 1883 and with the growth of suburban traffic, powers were granted to electrify the line in 1900. However, nothing was done until a Government Loan Guarantee Act in 1935 provided for electrification and a new service started in 1938, run jointly by the LMS and the Mersey Railway. The wooden stock seen in the 'past' picture , on July 8 1954, was painted in BR green and lasted until 1956 when new units were introduced. Currently, the services are operated by Class 508 units, as shown (right) on November 12 1987, with No.508 108 working from West Kirby to Liverpool Central. *Neville Knight/JCH.*

SEACOMBE & EGREMONT is a railway location of which no trace remains today. The station dates back to the latter part of the 19th century and was operated by a number of early companies which included The Seacombe, Hoylake & Deeside Railway, followed by the simpler Wirral Railway Company and was absorbed into the Great Central Railway in 1905. The LNER subsequently took over, the route giving this Company its only line into Wales.

Above: 'N5' 0-6-2T No. 69290 with a train to Wrexham Central in 1954. The station closed in 1960, with trains terminating at Bidston, where connections could be made for Birkenhead and Liverpool. The Bidston-Wrexham service continues to this day. The station site of has been completely redeveloped with modern housing, as pictured on November 12 1987.

Hugh Ballantyne /JCH.

NEW BRIGHTON: Part of the busy network in North Wirral, New Brighton station was opened in 1888 by the Wirral Railway Company. The picture taken on August 26 1966 (top) shows a DMU on the left, bound for Chester, whilst the Liverpool train on the right is a third rail EMU. In 1988, New Brighton's only passenger service was the frequent Liverpool service, using modern stock. On March 23 1988 (above) a pair of Class 508 units are flanking the shortened concrete canopy. *John Marshall/JCH.*

CALDY: LMS 2-6-2T No.40101 passes Caldy with a Hooton train around the time of closure of this station, in 1954. Note the GWR stock. The abandoned and overgrown appearance of this location today provides a sad contrast with the timber platform and neat permanent way of the 'past' picture. *Neville Knight/JCH.*

THURSTASTON. A single line staff change takes place as a West Kirby-bound train passes the station. The station buildings have now gone and the vegetation has grown considerably, but the site is still easily identified and houses the Thurstaston Visitor Centre of the Wirral Country Park. This Park was established in 1969, when the branch became part of the Wirral Way, and it is now possible to walk most of the 12 miles - with breaks at Neston and Heswall. *Neville Knight/JCH.*

KIRBY PARK : Close to West Kirby was Kirby Park station, a timber-built structure which has now been demolished. In the 'past' picture, GWR 2-6-2T No. 4124 is making haste with an afternoon train from West Kirby to Hooton, in August 1954. An enduring image of the country railway. *Neville Knight.*

Left: The sad spectacle greeting the visitor today at Kirby Park. Nature is slowly but steadily reclaiming the site, and only a footpath survives where the trains once ran. *JCH.*

NESTON: Situated on the western side of the Wirral, on the line from Bidston to Wrexham Central, Neston opened for business on May 18 1896, two months after goods trains started running. Right: On June 26 1949, GCR 'C13' No. 67429 arrives with a Seacombe-Wrexham 'local.' *Neville Fields.*

Below: A return visit to Neston today reveals that the Up platform has been extended across the site of the timber crossing, but the signal box has been demolished. The local pasenger service survives, and on March 23 1988, a Class 108 Derby 'lightweight' DMU with No. M54275 leading, drifts into the platform. *JCH.*

THE WREXHAM AREA

WREXHAM GENERAL:
Wrexham's principal station, 'General,' opened in 1846, linking the town with Chester. The station subsequently became part of the GWR on the important route from Shrewsbury to Birkenhead. It was a busy freight centre, and the GWR also had a roundhouse engine shed at Croes Newydd, just south of the station. Above: GWR 'Castle' No.5070 *Sir Daniel Gooch* approaches on April 18 1960, with the 6.20pm Chester-Shrewsbury train. *Michael Mensing*

Left: In 1988, there are no booked locomotive hauled passenger trains on the route(except Sunday diversions) which is reduced to single line between Chester and Wrexham. A Class 101 DMU, forming the 1218 Chester-Shrewsbury train, is pictured on December 8 1987. *JCH*

WREXHAM EXCHANGE is on the Bidston to Wrexham Central line, adjacent to General (GWR) station. Originally a terminus when opened in 1866, it became a through station in 1887 when the extension to Central was completed. It became part of the LNER in 1923, giving an interesting comparison between locomotives using the two neighbouring stations. *Michael Mensing.*

Above: A Derby 'lightweight' DMU, complete with yellow 'cats whiskers' is seen on April 18 1960, as the 3.55pm from Chester Northgate, bound for Central. Right: On June 2 1988, a Metro-Cammell DMU takes the same route, the line now reduced to a single track, served by a single, rather run-down platform. The name 'Exchange' has disappeared and the two stations are referred to as 'General'. *JCH.*

WREXHAM CENTRAL opened in 1887, as an extension from Exchange station and brought the railway right into the town. Services from Chester Northgate commenced in 1889 worked by the MS&L, which was later acquired by the GCR and finally absorbed into the LNER. The Cambrian was also involved at Central, which became a through station in 1895, when the Wrexham & Ellesmere line opened. The Ellesmere line closed in 1962 and the station reverted to being a terminus.

Above: BR Standard 2MT 2-6-2T No.84004 stands at one of the bay platforms, having worked the 2pm from Chester, in August 1955. The two bays were later obliterated by a car park. Just one platform remains in use, as shown on July 29 1987, with a Class 142 Pacer unit working the Bidston service. Even the elegant church spire has been demolished and all that remains to 'locate' the two pictures is the small steeple on the right.
Brian Morrison/JCH.

HIGHTOWN HALT (near Wrexham) was opened in 1923 and was a classic GWR-style country halt. Above: On Easter Monday, April 18 1960, GWR '1400' class 0-4-2T No. 1438 is in command of the 4.20pm Ellesmere-Wrexham auto-train service. This line was closed in 1962 and today the trackbed serves only as a walkway, as shown in the latter-day view, on October 17 1987. *Michael Mensing/JCH.*

BANGOR-ON-DEE: GWR '1400' class 0-4-2T No.1458, with auto-trailer No. W231W in tow, pauses at Bangor-on-Dee, between Ellesmere and Wrexham Central, on June 8 1962. No passengers are in evidence and the sleepy atmosphere makes it hardly surprising to learn that the line was closed later in the same year. Today, only a goods shed and one platform remain, and although the trees on the horizon are clearly recognisable, there is little else to indicate that the iron road ever came here. *N. R. Knight/JCH.*

ELLESMERE is a small country town, and was served by the railway from 1863, when the first section of the Oswestry Ellesmere & Whitchurch Railway opened between the latter two towns. Completion to Oswestry followed in 1864, when it also became part of the Cambrian system. In 1895, the Wrexham Central line opened, making Ellesmere a junction.

Right: Ivatt '2MT' 2-6-0 No.46516 (allocated to 6E - Wrexham) is working a Whitchurch to Welshpool train on October 30 1964. The station building stands to this day (below) although now in use as offices. The modern picture was taken on August 18 1987.
John Marshall/JCH.

SHOTTON (HIGH LEVEL) is on the Bidston (Wirral)-Wrexham Central GCR line. This is a true interchange, for the low level platforms are on the Chester-Holyhead main line and the two levels are connected. The booking office is on the high level Down side platform from where access is also gained to Shotton town centre. At the time the old picture (above) was taken, on April 18 1953, with LNER Class N5 0-6-2T No. 69349 leaving for Wrexham, there was a swing bridge crossing the River Dee, controlled from a high cabin, just discernible beyond the down platform. This was removed when the old bridge was replaced. *Neville Fields.*

Above : The wooden platforms have given way to more modern material and the old buildings replaced by a less attractive brick structure. A Class 101 Metro-Cammell DMU pauses with the 1520 service from Hawarden Bridge to Wrexham. *JCH.*

HOPE & PENYFFORDD, between Chester and Mold, was just one of four stations including the name 'Hope' at one time or another, despite the sparse settlement in the area. Above: LMS Fairburn 2-6-4T No. 42209 stops with the 7.30pm Ruthin-Chester General, on April 28 1962, the last Up train to call at this station before closure. *Michael Mensing.*

Right : Hope & Peny-ffordd, on August 31 1987. The semaphore signals in the garden, occupying the former trackbed, provide a nos-talgic flavour. The building was being used as a Wool Shop. *JCH.*

RUABON: On the once-busy GWR main line from Chester to Shrewsbury, '43xx' class 2-6-0 No. 7309 is seen just south of Ruabon, with an Up freight, on August 9 1956. At that time the Ruabon district generated considerable freight traffic from local collieries and other industrial installations, and Ruabon was also the junction for the lines to Llangollen, Corwen and Barmouth. *Brian Morrison.*

Below: Nowadays, Ruabon's only railway facility is an unstaffed halt on BR's Chester-Shrewsbury line, served by a roughly two-hourly service in each direction. In the Summer 1988 timetable, the majority of trains were booked for Class 150 Sprinter units. On September 26 1987, No. 150146, is working the 1218 Chester-Shrewsbury service. *PDS.*

CHIRK, like Ruabon, lies between Wrexham and Gobowen on the former GWR main line. Our 'sixties' scene (above) depicts GWR 4-6-0 'Hall' No. 6910 *Gossington Hall,* storming through the station with an Up freight on October 13 1962. *Ian Holt.*

Right: A Derby Class 108 DMU calls to set down a handful of passengers at the same location on September 26 1987. The station is now unstaffed, but at least the Up platform shelter has been designed in keeping with the railway environment. The industry beyond the trees is the Kronospan plant, where new railway facilities were installed in late 1988 for incoming timber traffic from Scotland. *PDS.*

NORTH SALOP

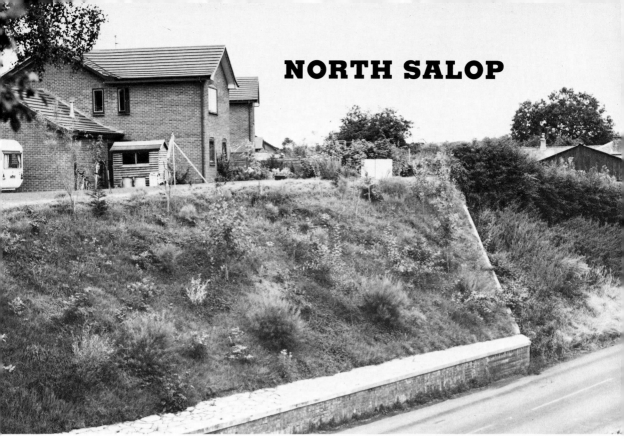

AUDLEM : A few miles south of Nantwich, Audlem was on the former GWR line to Wellington. The origins of the route date back to the Nantwich & Market Drayton Railway, incorporated in 1861 and completed two years later, being absorbed by the GWR in 1897. Considered very much a secondary line, it enjoyed a flurry of activity during electrification of the WCML. Below : LMR 2-6-2T No.41241 (carrying an 84A shed plate - Stafford Road shed, Wolverhampton) leaves with a Crewe train. This locomotive is preserved on the Keighley & Worth Valley Railway. *Hugh Ballantyne.*

Above: Since closure in 1963, Audlem station has been obliterated and the bridge formerly straddling the station has been removed. It is difficult to believe that it is the same location. August 29 1987. *JCH.*

ADDERLEY was the first station from Market Drayton towards Nantwich, on the line from Wellington. Above: Ivatt 2-6-2T No.41232 is entering the station with the 5.18pm train from Crewe, on August 12 1961. The course of the railway is now barely discernible, but very careful scrutiny of the modern view (August 8 1987) reveals that the remains of the waiting shelter can be seen peeping through the undergrowth! *Michael Mensing/JCH.*

HODNET : The GWR origins of the line from Nantwich to Wellington are clear as 'Hall' 4-6-0 No. 4943 *Marrington Hall* arrives on April 15 1963 with the 12.15 pm Wellington-Crewe train. Hodnet closed the same year and no trace of the platforms or buildings remain, but the goods shed still stands (the site being used as a coal yard), as seen in the picture taken on August 29 1987. An interesting historical note is that at one time, because the GWR service was so sparse, the North Staffordshire Railway was allowed to run trains to Hodnet from Market Drayton on market days!
Michael Mensing/JCH.

MARKET DRAYTON was on the line beteween Nantwich and Wellington, and following the original Nantwich & Market Drayton Railway's connection with the Wellington & Drayton Railway in 1867, the GWR enjoyed access to the LNWR at Nantwich and thence to Crewe. The NSR also reached Market Drayton in 1870 with its route from Newcastle-under-Lyme and Stoke, making this small market town into a junction. The NSR line closed to passengers in 1956, but the line from Wellington to Nantwich remained open for passenger traffic until 1963; complete closure followed in 1967.

Above: '2MT' 2-6-2T No.41232 is seen leaving the station on April 15 1963 with a Wellington-Crewe train. The site is very different today (right). A number of buildings remained on August 29 1987. *Michael Mensing/JCH*

WHITCHURCH: A reminder that the locomotives introduced to displace steam have now themselves passed into history. With steam blowing from the safety valves of its train heating boiler, English Electric Type 4 D213, *Andania* (subsequently 40013) heads a Down express through the station on September 9 1963, just four years after entering service. *Michael Mensing.*

Above : The same view on August 29 1987. The trackwork has been simplified, the station modernised and the semaphores have all gone, but a few Up side sidings remain and the line between Crewe and Shrewsbury is still quite busy with local services, through trains to Cardiff from both Manchester and Holyhead, together with regular freight and parcels trains. A Class 118 DMU, forming the 1030 Pembroke Dock-Crewe, is passing stored MSV four-wheel stone wagons. *JCH.*

OSWESTRY & BORDER BRANCHES

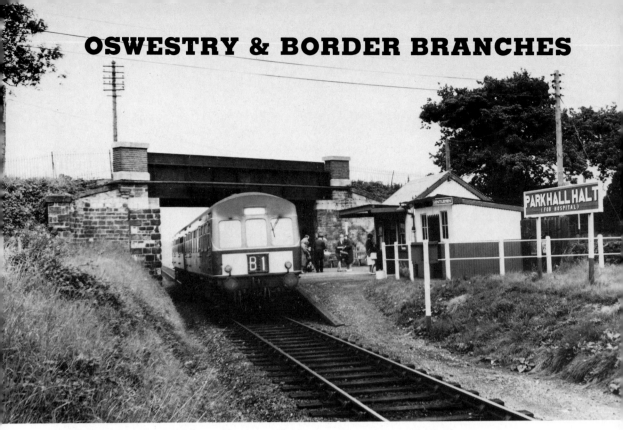

PARK HALL was the only intermediate halt on the 2 1/2-miles Gobowen-Oswestry branch, built by the Shrewsbury & Chester Railway in 1848 and subsequently absorbed by the GWR. Passenger services on this branch outlived those on the Cambrian line through Oswestry by nearly two years; the last train left Oswestry for Gobowen on November 7 1966. During the last year of operation, a Metropolitan-Cammell DMU arrives at Park Hall, bound for **Oswestry.** *Hugh Ballantyne.*

Above : The platform is still discernible at Park Hall, where a new 'fixed distant' board (on the left) warns the drivers of Blodwel ballast trains that they are approaching the junction at Gobowen. September 26 1987. *PDS.*

OSWESTRY (1) : In the fork between the diverging Gobowen and Whitchurch lines lay Oswestry's substantial GWR engine shed. The shed is illustrated (above) on October 30 1964, with LMS Ivatt 2-6-0s Nos. 46512, 46514, 46516 and 46515 in attendance. *John Marshall.*

Below: This is the equivalent view in September 1987, by which time much of the site had been redeveloped for light industrial use. *PDS.*

OSWESTRY (2) : Twelve years elapsed between the arrival of Oswestry's first railway (from Gobowen) and the opening in 1860 of the line from Oswestry to Welshpool, later to become part of the Cambrian Railways' main line. But it was the Cambrian Railways which transformed Oswestry, from a quiet country town into a hive of industrial activity. A locomotive and carriage works was constructed here in 1863, and the town was also chosen (despite its location in England) as the Cambrian's headquarters. The former Cambrian station at Oswestry is pictured (below) on May 18 1963, with BR Ivatt 2-6-0 No. 46515 arriving from Gobowen. Oswestry lost its through services on the Welshpool-Whitchurch axis in January 1965, leaving only the Gobowen-Oswestry 'shuttle' in operation until November 1966. *Ian Holt.*

Below: No trace remains of the Down side buildings at Oswestry in 1988, and the edge of the former Down platform is engulfed in undergrowth. At the time of writing, a Blodwel-Bescot ballast train is scheduled to polish the surviving rails each weekday, but at the time of going to press, this train was thought unlikely to continue beyond Autumn 1988. *PDS.*

OSWESTRY (3) : BR 2-6-4T No. 80104 stands in the Cambrian station at Oswestry with a Welshpool-bound passenger working on October 30 1964. *John Marshall.*

Below: Although the GWR terminus at Oswestry was razed to the ground to make way for a new bus station, the neighbouring Cambrian Railways station has experienced much less drastic treatment, and the Company's imposing headquarters building still stands, as illustrated here on September 27 1987. Notwithdstanding this, the once-extensive station is now a derelict shadow of its former self. *PDS.*

LLANFYLLIN was the terminus of the Cambrian Railways' most substantial branch in the Shropshire/ Montgomeryshire border district. Traffic was particularly buoyant during construction of Lake Vyrnwy reservoir in the 1880s. Above: LMS 2-6-0 No. 46512 is pictured arriving at Llanfyllin with the 12.55 pm service from Llanymynech on October 5 1963. The branch had then almost reached the end of its life, for freight facilities were withdrawn in 1964 and passenger services ceased in 1965. *Michael Mensing.*

Right: The same viewpoint on September 27 1987, showing the light industry which has recently sprung up on the station site. Both the main station building and the goods shed have been incorporated into the development pictured here. *PDS.*

LLANRHAEADR MOCHNANT : The Tanat Valley Light Railway from Blodwel Junction to Llangynog was opened in 1904, following a number of abortive attempts to bring both standard and narrow gauge railways into the district. Passenger services on the branch lasted just 47 years, for they were suspended during a national coal shortage in 1951 and never restored. Goods were carried up the branch as far as Llanrhaeadr Mochnant until December 1960, and this attractive scene depicts GWR 0-6-0PT No. 1603, about to depart from Llanrhaeadr with a 'pick-up goods' in 1958. *Neville Knight.*

Below: Only a shed and the distant outline of the Berwyn hills remain to locate the same spot today, as recorded here on September 27 1987. *PDS.*

RURAL CLWYD

BODFARI: The Mold & Denbigh Junction Railway opened in 1869, worked by the LNWR, and it operated for almost 100 years until passenger traffic ceased in 1962. Bodfari was the end of a double track section and in the 'past' picture, taken during 1961, Riddles 2-6-0 No.78056 is running tender-first towards Denbigh. *Neville Knight.*

Top right : The station today presents a very different image. The building itself is well maintained, but the platforms and trackbed has been levelled and taken over for use by caravans. *JCH.*

DENBIGH was once a busy railway centre, boasting a small locomotive shed and was the junction of the lines from Rhyl to the north and from Mold to the east. The line to Corwen ran to the south. The LMS timetable of 1947 shows a regular service from Chester.

Below left: LMS 2-6-4T No.42431 is pictured with two LMS non-corridor coaches forming a Chester train in 1960. In the background is MR '2F' 0-6-0 No.58293. The station was closed in 1962 and the modern picture, taken on October 17 1987, shows that a number of railway buildings are still in use. *N.R. Knight/JCH.*

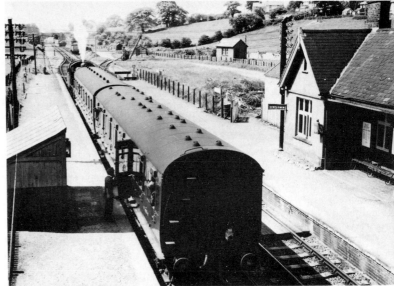

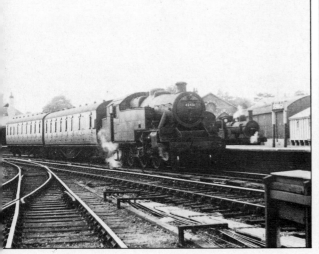

RUTHIN : There was a time when the GWR had aspirations of access to the lucrative North Wales coast market, with a route from Corwen to Rhyl, but this was not to be. The original Vale of Clwyd Railway was incorporated in 1856, followed by the Denbigh Ruthin & Corwen Railway, the line being worked by the LNWR, which commenced services from Denbigh to Ruthin in 1862 and assumed control by 1866.

Above: Riddles 2-6-0 No.78056 at Ruthin station in 1961, with a Denbigh service. The line closed in 1962 and the station area was subsequently re-developed, as shown on October 17 1987. Nothing remains of the railway in this view, but nearby is a yard crane, mounted on a plinth as a permanent reminder of Ruthin's railway past.
N R Knight/JCH.

CAERWYS: The line from Chester to Corwen ran through delightful countryside, serving many small communities as well as the larger towns of Mold, Denbigh and Ruthin. Caerwys is about seven miles east of Denbigh and had several sidings, laid in 1901 for the local cement works. Right: On April 21 1962, Riddles Class 4-6-0 No.75010 pulls away from the station with a Denbigh-Chester train. Closed in 1962, the station building survives as the offices of a timber mill, as indicated by the logs in the picture taken on January 28 1988.
N.R. Knight/JCH.

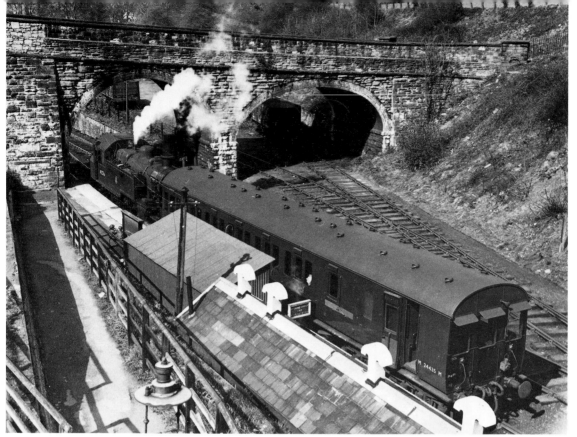

HOLYWELL TOWN was at the end of the short branch from the main line at Holywell Junction, and on April 4 1953, Ivatt '2MT' No. 41276 stands at the terminus in charge of motor train No. M24435M. This was the shuttle service to Holywell Junction, less than two miles distant. In 1947, the journey took just eight minutes, including a stop at St Winefrides Halt, the only intermediate station. *Neville Knight.*

Below: Passenger traffic ended in 1954 and the junction was removed four years later. Of Holywell station itself, little remains, although the platform edging is still discernible beneath the bridge. Now in use as a public park, the modern picture shows the scene on October 17 1987. *JCH.*

LLONG station was a
few miles south east of
Mold, on the line to
Chester. Opened in 1849,
the line survived until
closure in 1962. In the
'past' view, Riddles Class
'4MT' No. 75010 is roll-
ing in with a two-coach
train forming the 6.35pm
from Chester General to
Ruthin on April 28 1962,
the last day of service. A
closure notice, common-
ly seen on rural stations
at this time, can be seen
posted to the right of the
train. *Michael Mensing.*

Below: Llong on August
14 1987, the track long
gone, but with the
station building - and
even a couple of name-
boards - still extant. *JCH.*

ACROSS THE HILLS
WREXHAM - BLAENAU

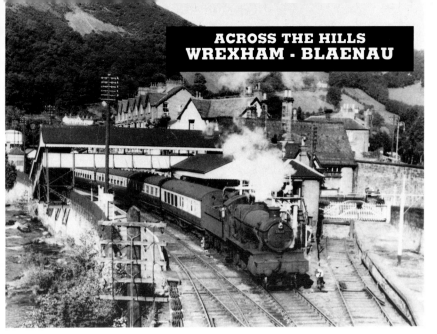

LLANGOLLEN, closed to pasengers in 1965, with freight services from Llandudno Goods Junction ceasing in 1968; the track was subsequently lifted. Passenger working by the Llangollen Railway Society were restored over a short section of track in 1981 and by Christmas 1985 trains were running again to Berwyn. Left: In the late 1950s, GWR 'Manor' No. 7822 *Foxcote Manor* is seen at Llangollen, where the locomotive is also preserved today, in working order. The modern picture was taken on June 19 1988. *Llangollen Railway Society/JCH*

TREVOR : GWR 'Manor' 4-6-0 No. 7811 *Dunley Manor* rolls into Trevor station, between Llangollen and Ruabon, with a Pwllheli-Birkenhead train, on October 13 1962. Through workings continued to use the Barmouth-Ruabon line to the end of its existence, in 1965. *Ian Holt.*

Below, right: Abandoned waste ground now occupies the site of Trevor station, with bushes and trees gradually encroaching upon the former trackbed towards Llangollen. The photograph is dated September 26 1987. *PDS.*

CORWEN: Within two years, three separate minor companies opened railway routes to Corwen: the Denbigh & Corwen Railway (1864), the Llangollen & Corwen Railway (1865) and finally the Corwen & Bala Railway (1866). The first of these became the LNWR Denbigh-Corwen branch, whilst the other two were soon amalgamated to form part of the GWR line from Ruabon to Dolgellau and (via Cambrian metals) Barmouth. Until 1927 Corwen had its own GWR engine shed as well as goods, exchange and carriage sidings. The demise of Corwen's railways was almost as rapid as their arrival: the LNWR branch closed in April 1962 (though there had been no regular passenger traffic since 1953), and total closure of the GWR route followed in December, hastened by several weeks. following flood damage.

Above: Corwen in 1963, as a GWR 0-6-0PT arrives from Llangollen, whilst the modern scene (below) shows the complete transformation which had taken place by August 10 1987. *Michael Mensing/PDS.*

LLANDRILLO was the second station from Corwen on the Barmouth line. Below: BR Class 4MT 4-6-0 No. 75026 leaves the loop at Llandrillo with the 1.35 pm Chester-Barmouth service on October 5 1963, 14 months before closure. Lower: The same location on August 10 1987, with the trackbed transformed into a timber yard, although the former goods shed still stands, just visible behind a more modern structure on the right. *Michael Mensing/PDS.*

TRAWSFYNYDD: The GWR branch from Bala Junction to Blaenau Ffestiniog crossed some of the wildest terrain traversed by any railway in Wales. Little business was generated at any of its intermediate stations, and when plans were announced in 1957 to flood part of the trackbed in the creation of a new reservoir (Llyn Celyn), the line's fate was effectively sealed. Regular passenger services ceased on January 2 1960, and the line closed completely just over a year later.

Our 'past' photograph shows the very last passenger train through Trawsfynydd, a Stephenson Locomotive Society enthusiasts excursion, which ran on January 22 1961. *John Marshall.*

Today, Trawsfynydd station has been lavishly incorporated into a private dwelling, as pictured on August 10 1987. The goods shed still stands, now in commercial use. Barely two miles north, the 'iron road' itself remains open, for regular BR freight trains conveying nuclear waste from Trawsfynydd Power Station. *PDS.*

BLAENAU FFESTINIOG: Around the village of Blaenau Ffestiniog, the mountain sides are clothed with the indelible marks of slate quarrying. This industry not only transformed large tracts of the Welsh landscape but was also instrumental in bringing railways to many of the country's remoter districts. During the latter half of the 19th century both the LNWR and the GWR forged their way over and through the hills to Blaenau. Separate stations were opened by the LNWR and the GWR, in 1881 and 1883, and although they lay on the same alignment there was never a physical connection between them in pre-Nationalisation days. The old photograph shows Blaenau Central (GWR) station in 1952, with 0-6-0PT No. 7440 on a branch working to Bala. *Hugh Ballantyne.*

Top: After passenger services ceased between Bala and Blaenau Ffestiniog in 1960, the GWR terminus was closed, leaving the LNWR station in use as the terminus of BR's Conwy Valley branch. In 1964, however, the GWR line between Blaenau and Trawsfynydd was re-opened for nuclear flask traffic, and a new stretch of line was built through Blaenau so that trains could - for the first time -

reach Trawsfynydd from the Conwy Valley. Then, in March 1982, BR passenger trains were extended over the 1964 link to the site of the GWR station, where new facilities were opened both for BR and for

the final extension of the rejuvenated Ffestiniog Railway. Below: The new interchange station on August 10 1987, with access between FR and BR platforms provided by footbridge. *PDS.*

THE CAMBRIAN COAST

BARMOUTH : The main part of Barmouth station was constructed on the north side of the level crossing but, shortly after the Cambrian system was amalgamated with the GWR in 1922, an extra Up bay platform was installed on the south side of the crossing. That bay is pictured here on October 24 1964, with Ivatt Class '2MT' 2-6-0 No. 46521 (now preserved on the Severn Valley Railway) awaiting departure to Dolgellau. *Neville Fields.*

Below: It's April 6 1988 and the track has long since been removed from Barmouth's bay, whilst the station loop has been shortened by moving the southernmost turnout nearer the crossing. Class 150/1 unit No. 150138 is approaching Barmouth whilst working the 1410 Machynlleth-Pwllheli service. The GWR signal box (on the left) is a listed structure and will remain in position after the introduction of radio signalling on this line. *PDS.*

AFON WEN: The first trains to reach Afon Wen were those of the Carnarvonshire Railway, whose services between Caernarfon and Afon Wen (continuing initially over Cambrian metals to Penrhyndeudraeth) commenced on September 2 1867. A month later, the Cambrian itself was in business as far as Pwllheli, and Afon Wen became a meeting place for the two companies and their descendants. There was little habitation in the vicinity of Afon Wen; it was similar in character to that loneliest and most isolated of Cambrian stations, Dovey Junction.

Below: Our April 1961 photograph shows Riddles 2-6-2T No. 82000 arriving with the 9.25am from Barmouth whilst GWR '2251' Class No. 2287 waits in the other platform with the 10.25am from Pwllheli. *R. E. James Robertson.*

Lower: The sad spectacle of Afon Wen on August 12 1987. A solitary platform edge survives as a reminder of busier and happier times past. *PDS.*

PWLLHELI : Pwllheli was the limit of the Cambrian Railways operations on the Lleyn Peninsula; plans to extend the tracks westwards to Nevin or Porth Dinllaen were never realised. The terminus opened in 1909, with two platform faces, plus berthing sidings on each side. The track layout and signalling survived relatively unscathed into the 1970s, as seen in the 'past' view, on March 28 1973. *Wyn Hobson.*

Above : Towards the end of the 1970s, rationalisation was begun in earnest, and Pwllheli's signal boxes were closed and with the exception of one platform line and one refuge siding, all track was removed. The modern view shows Pwllheli on August 12 1987. *PDS.*

AROUND CAERNARFON

NANTLLE was the terminus of Carnarvonshire's first railway: as early as 1828 horse-drawn trams were carrying slate from Nantlle's extensive mines along a 3ft 6in gauge line, just over nine miles in length, to the quayside at Caernarfon. In 1872, the section between Penygroes and Nantlle was converted to standard gauge, several years after the remainder of the line (from Penygroes to Caernarfon) had been incorporated into the Caernarfon-Afon Wen line and similarly upgraded. The change of gauge between Penygroes and Nantlle did not eliminate the need for exchange sidings at Nantlle, however, since the quarry lines were of 2'0" gauge to begin with and remained so after the change. The exchange sidings are illustrated (below) in 1952 with both 2ft gauge and standard gauge wagons present. *Hugh Ballantyne.*

Above: The Nantlle branch remained open for goods traffic until December 2 1963, since when part of the trackbed has been converted into a relief road and the station area into a children's playground. The 'present' view is dated August 11 1987. *PDS.*

LLANBERIS BRANCH: Although there already existed a narrow gauge railway linking the slate mines of Llanberis with the sea at Port Dinorwic, the LNWR was also successful in bringing a standard gauge line from Caernarfon to Llanberis in 1869, taking a picturesque route via Pont Rug and Cwm-y-Glo. Regular passenger services lasted only until 1930, after which excursion and goods trains were the line's only source of revenue. In the 'past' photograph, taken three years before final closure of the line, Stanier 2-6-4T No. 42489 is seen leaving Llanberis with the Up 'Snowdonian' of September 6 1961. *Ian Holt.*

Above: The same location on April 7 1988; the trackbed in use partly as a lakeside footpath and partly as a road. *PDS.*

LLANBERIS STATION: Goods trains continued to serve Llanberis until September 7 1964, when the branch was closed completely. Above: Stanier 2-6-4T No. 42489 shunts the last goods train at Llanberis. The station building survives, as a restaurant and craft centre, as pictured (below) on April 7 1988. *Barry Wynne/PDS.*

CAERNARFON: For a short period, Caernarfon boasted three terminal stations: one for Bangor, another for Llanberis, and a third for the line to Afon Wen. Only the Bangor & Carnarvon Railway station survived beyond 1870, however, and this remained in use until the cessation of passenger services from Bangor a century later. The interesting scene (above) depicts the south end of Caernarfon in April 1966, complete with intricate track layout, signalling and station furniture. Class 5MT No. 45282 is shunting after recovering materials from the Llanberis branch - hence the signalling components visible in the nearest wagon. Nothing remains
Barry Wynne.

CAERNARFON (BANGOR LINE) : The stub of the Bangor-Afon Wen line, between Bangor and Caernarfon, was singled in 1966, closed to goods traffic in 1969, and closed to passengers on January 5 1970. The line's usefulness was not yet finished, however. Following the Britannia Bridge fire of May 1970 (see also page 99), Caernarfon was chosen as a temporary container terminal to replace the inaccessible facility at Holyhead, and so the branch enjoyed regular train services again from June 15 1970 until February 5 1972. Above: The simplified layout north of Caernarfon on December 27 1968, with a two-car Gloucester RCW DMU forming the 1200 train to Bangor. Below: The same viewpoint, August 11 1987. *Wyn Hobson/PDS.*

PORT SIDING: Fairburn Class 4 2-6-4T No. 42077 (above) heads south near Port Siding, between Bangor and Caernarfon, with a fine selection of vintage coaching stock, on September 6 1961. The train is the 8.25am 'through' working from Liverpool to Pwllheli, an attractive journey which involved a reversal at Afon Wen in order to reach the former Cambrian terminus. *Ian Holt.*

Above: Today, the location is barely recognisable, but for the slope of a distant hillside, as pictured here in August 1987. *PDS.*

ANGLESEY

HOLYHEAD : This station dates back from 1880, by which time the port was already busy handling Anglo-Irish passenger and freight traffic. Also opened in 1880 was the imposing station hotel, seen in the background of our 'past' picture (below) of a Class 108 DMU arriving to work the 1634 Holyhead-Bangor 'local' on July 23 1973. The hotel closed in 1951, but stood for a further 30 years, until the site was required for new railway passenger facilities. Our 'present' picture, taken on June 16 1988, shows Class 47/4 No. 47571 backing out of the platform whilst pilot locomotive No. 08921 shunts coaching stock for the next InterCity service to London. In the harbour (behind the site of the old hotel) is the Irish Sea ferry *St. Columba* which has just arrived from Ireland.
Wyn Hobson/JCH.

HOLYHEAD SHED : Steam-hauled expresses continued to serve Holyhead until 1967. This Summer 1962 photograph at Holyhead MPD shows a mixture of LMS and BR standard types on parade: actual identities are LMS Class 5MT 4-6-0 Nos. 45116 and 44712 and BR 'Britannia' 4-6-2 No. 70047 - the only un-named member of this class. The approach tracks to the station and harbour run just to the left of the signal box; the station hotel is glimpsed through the open shed doors. *Barry Wynne*

Below: In 1988, Holyhead motive power depot is reduced in status to a fuelling and stabling point for locomotives and DMUs. Its only residents are a pair of Class 08 shunting locomotives utilised in the station and harbour areas, and even these are nominally maintained at Crewe. On April 7 1988, the only motive power present was a Class 142 *Pacer* unit, standing to the left of the shed, and a shunter, stabled out of sight behind the photographer. *PDS.*

AMLWCH was connected to the Chester & Holyhead Railway via a 16-mile branch from Gaerwen. Above: The neat and well-kept station at Amlwch on April 7 1961, with a two-car Derby-built DMU (in original livery) waiting to depart on the 2.05pm service to Bangor. Passenger services were withdrawn in December 1964, but the line has been kept alive since then with freight trains serving the Associated Octel factory at Amlwch.

This factory was connected to BR metals in 1952 by means of a 3/4-mile light railway, diverging just outside the 'throat' of the passenger station. No trace of the terminus survived on August 11 1987, when the 'present' picture was taken. A new road cuts across the former trackbed nowadays, and part of the goods yard area has passed into commercial use, involving extensions to the surviving corrugated iron goods shed.
R. E. James-Robertson/PDS.

LLANGEFNI was one of five intermediate stations on the Amlwch branch. **Above:** On April 7 1961, LMS Ivatt '2MT' 2-6-2T No. 41233 is waiting to depart from Llangefni goods yard whilst the signals show 'all clear' for an Amlwch-bound passenger working. **Below:** The remaining single track on August 11 1987, with the loop and goods yard long since removed and now heavily overgrown. *R.E. James-Robertson/PDS.*

GAERWEN: A delightful rural railway scene at Gaerwen (above) as LMS Class 5MT 4-6-0 No. 45345 clatters over the Amlwch branch junction, with the 12.22 Holyhead-Llandudno Junction train on April 7 1961. On the right is a rake of cattle wagons, possibly bound for Holyhead for another consignment of Irish beef! The Holyhead-Chester cattle traffic was the last of its kind on BR and survived (just!) into the 1970s. *R.E. James-Robertson.*

Above: The same view on August 11 1987. Gaerwen station was closed in February 1966, although its signal box survives to control the level crossing and access to the Amlwch branch. The track layout has been rationalised and Amlwch-bound freight trains must first set back over a crossover before proceeding along the branch. *PDS.*

LLANFAIRPWLLGWYNGYLL-
GOGERYCHWRYNDROBWLLL-
LANTYSILIOGOGOGOCH, as Victorian whimsy would have us know it (Llanfair PG is more manageable!) was the first permanent station to be opened on Anglesey. Regular services began on August 1 1848 to a temporary station at Holyhead, initially with a coach connection from Llanfair PG to the mainland, via Telford's suspension bridge over the Menai Strait. Not until 1850, upon the opening of Stephenson's Britannia Tubular Bridge (see page 99), were through rail services possible from Anglesey to Bangor and beyond. Llanfair PG. station succumbed to the Beeching axe on February 14 1966, along with 11 other stations between Chester and Holyhead. But closure was short-lived. During the reconstruction of the Britannia Bridge, between 1970 and 1972, Llanfair PG became a temporary terminus once again, with a DMU shuttle service from Holyhead. The old photograph (below) shows the modest facilities during this period: a Park Royal Class 103 DMU is just arriving at the temporary platform on

the afternoon of August 19 1970. This temporary re-instatement to the railway system was followed by a permanent re-opening, from May 7 1973, with new platforms and nameboards.

Below: Class 150/1 Sprinter No. 150128, operating the 1306 Holyhead-Bangor service of August 11 1987. In the background are the town's tourist centre and car and coach park . *Wyn Hobson/PDS.*

BRITANNIA TUBULAR BRIDGE: On March 5 1850, the first train ran through Robert Stephenson's magnificent and innovative Tubular Bridge across the Menai Strait. For 120 years the structure performed a vital role in transporting passengers, mail and goods to and from the port of Holyhead. The 'past' photograph shows the eastern portal of the bridge on October 29 1966, with English Electric Type 4 locomotive No. D311 (later Class 40 No. 40111) heading the 1140 Holyhead-London Euston service. *Wyn Hobson.*

Above: During the night of May 23 1970, the Britannia Bridge was rendered unusable by a ravaging fire, which produced spectacular pictures on news broadcasts. The stone towers survived intact but the original iron tubes were twisted and weakened beyond repair. With the healthy traffic levels prevailing at the time, not to mention the recent investment in Holyhead's container port, there was no serious possibility of closing the line, and a new steel-arched structure was built as a matter of urgency, and opened on January 30 1972. Only a single track was laid across the new bridge, though there is sufficient width for a second track to be added if required. Provision was also made for a road deck to be placed on top of the new railway bridge, and this was duly installed during the late 1970s, with the aim of relieving congestion on Telford's original road bridge. The 'new look' Britannia Bridge on August 11 1987, with cars and lorries out of sight, yet only a few feet above the photographer's head! *PDS.*

THE NORTH WALES COAST MAIN LINE

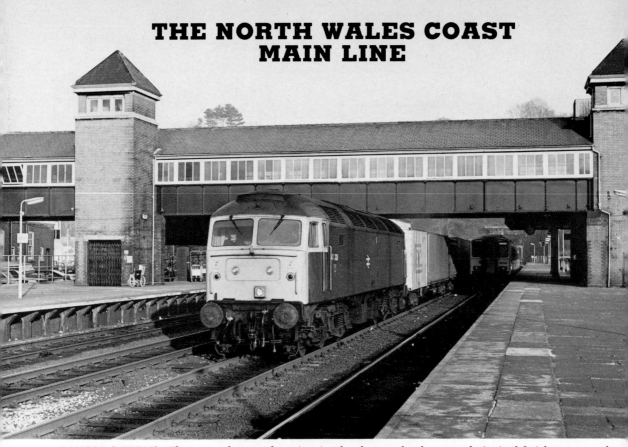

BANGOR (MIDDLE): These two photographs epitomise the changes that have revolutionised freight transport by rail in the past few decades. Below : LYR 0-6-0 No.12269 trundles through Bangor with a short loose-coupled goods train, complete with guard's van at the rear, whilst the modern picture (above) shows Class 47 No. 47338 heading the daily 75mph *Freightliner* service from Birmingham to Holyhead, laden with containers for shipment to Ireland. The photographs are dated July 9 1947 and April 6 1988 respectively. *Neville Knight/PDS.*

LLANDUDNO JUNCTION (LLANDUDNO BRANCH): The geographical position of Llandudno precluded its incorporation into the Chester-Holyhead main line. A branch to serve Llandudno had to be built along the eastern side of the Conwy estuary, joining the main line at what was then a wayside location between Conwy and Mochdre. The main North Wales coast road crossed the Llandudno branch adjacent to its junction with the main line and our 'past' view shows a DMU passing over the crossing in August 1966, with Llandudno Junction station off to the left. *Wyn Hobson.*

Left: This level crossing became a road bottleneck and eventually a bridge was built, radically changing this scene, as shown on August 10 1987. Now, even the road pictured here is considered obsolete, for earthworks were much in evidence in 1988 for a tunnel under the Conwy estuary. *PDS.*

LLANDUDNO JUNCTION (EAST END): BR Class 5 4-6-0 No. 73011 arrives at Llandudno Junction, dating from 1897, with a Down Summer Saturday 'extra' on August 6 1966. Semaphore signals and other station adornments give the scene a fine 'period' appearance. The station had six through lines, with bays and sidings. *Wyn Hobson.*

Above: Two Class 150/2 *Sprinter* units arrive at the same location on August 10 1987, forming the 1151 Hull-Holyhead service. Colour light signals are now controlled from a new box at the west end of the station, and passenger services are concentrated on the extended island platform illustrated here. *PDS.*

COLWYN BAY : The four track main line had already been rationalised when this photograph (above) of a Park Royal DMU on a Chester-Bangor working was taken on July 24 1973. These distinctive DMUs were once common in North and Mid Wales, but withdrawal was well under way by the late 1970s and the last example was taken out of service in 1983. *Wyn Hobson.*

Nowadays, the railway between Colwyn Bay and Llandudno Junction is parallelled by the A55 trunk road, a scheme which cost £500 million and results in much unwelcome competition for the North Wales Coast main line. Below: On August 10 1987, *Sprinters* Nos. 150227 and 150221 form the 1536 Crewe-Llandudno Junction service. *PDS.*

DYSERTH: Built to serve the lead and haematite mines in the Prestatyn Valley, the single track three-miles branch to Dyserth opened in 1869. From 1905, a passenger service was running from Prestatyn. By 1928 five intermediate halts had been added. Passenger services ended in 1930 but freight traffic continued until 1964, the line subsequently surviving as a private siding until 1973.

Right: LMS '4F' No. 44367 at Dyserth in May 1958. On February 25 1988, (below) the goods shed still stood but nature had reclaimed the trackbed.
Neville Knight/JCH.